Once again, we will dance…

Tanya McDonald

BookLeaf
Publishing

Presentation by *BookLeaf Publishing*

Web: www.bookleafpub.com

E-mail: info@bookleafpub.com

ISBN: 9789357691406

First edition 2022

DEDICATION

To L, T and T ~ May you know I always tried.

To S ~ For returning.

One Day

One day
They will no longer
Want a goodbye kiss
From you
At the school gate

One day
They will no longer
Call for your help
With a soapy hair wash

One day
They will no longer
Jump into your bed
For tickles and cuddles

One day
You will realise
That you are no longer
The mother
You once needed to be

Elusivity

I read until the wee hours
Until my eyes are so heavy
There is no other option
Than for sleep to find me

Wonder

3

I wonder if the tea
Wonders whose lips
It will pass

Friend or Foe

You never know what is going on in the
background
Who is thinking fondly of you
Who is working towards your demise
Who is building on your relationship
Who is quietly retreating
And who is actively about to tear you apart

Anguish

5

I don't know who you are
But I think of you often
The husband whose wife never made it home
The child who sits and waits for the daddy who
never comes
The mother whose heart has an irreparable gash
From the 'what if's' and the 'if only's'
I don't know who you are
But I think of you often

Expectations

'Did you expect something from me?'
He asked
'Yes, I fucking had expectations of you!'
I expected phone calls, not one a year, on my
birthday at 11pm,
When you remembered
And I had given up, after waiting all day
Any hope that you loved me slipping away
As the minutes passed
'Yes, I had fucking expectations!'
I expected that you'd know me,
My favourite colour,
My friends, my fears
I deserved your protection.
I expected your protection.
Shouldn't that have been at minimum?
So yes, I expected many things of you
Of which none that you delivered

Cyclical

It was you who taught me
To be submissive
Please them, fear them
It was you who taught me
To do the things they wanted me to do
It was you who taught me
To do whatever it took
To placate him
It was you who told me to never turn down
Any of their requests
Not to hurt their feelings
Or to anger them
It was you who taught me
How to be abused
But it is me
Middle aged
Still practising
It is me
Learning how to say no
Without fear or trepidation
It is me
Implementing boundaries
For me
Because you wouldn't
Or maybe you were never taught how

It is me
Saying
Enough is enough

Mirror, mirror

I grew up in fear
Your size
Your words
Your anger
Your violence
Volatile
A smashed window here
A thrown plate there
And now,
As the ambulance is called for you
I see a child's fear
Not in my eyes
But yours

I see you

The girl who hides behind her books
The boy lost in his computer game world
The child who grows their hair long to hide
behind it

I see you

The girl who stands back at the lockers
The boy who lashes out
The child who gets frustrated because they don't
understand

I see you

The girl who doesn't want to go home
The boy who does
The children trying to find their way
In a world the adults are still trying to find theirs

I see you

The End Is The Beginning

This pain
Pain
Mental preparation
Uncontrollable urge to push
The baby hurt
Really hurt
Trying to come through
Mental strength
No-one prepared me for what I was experiencing
And left me… bewildered.
Pushing, a blur
Mental and physical agony
Frightened, scared
A good mother
Loving, leaving
Lovingly reassured
Foolish, lost
Fighting strength
A nomad wandering
Pressure, PRESSURE
Waiting, waiting
Pushing, pushing
The baby's heartbeat
In the shower
Screaming
'JUST GET IT OUT!'

Rain falls softly on the town… (Inspired by Verlaine and Rimbaud)

Tears don't spill onto my cheek
As sunlight falls on the city;
What strength, what splendour
Does so enter my mind!

Oh, hard sight of the sun
On the ground, in the ocean!
For a mind that knows pleasure
Of the silence of the sunlight.

Tears don't fall without great cause
In this mind at ease
No faithfulness, no gain?
This delight has no cause

And it is the greatest pain
That I can tell you why
With love, with ruin,
My mind feels no pain!

The Piano Kissed by a Frail Hand… (Inspired by Verlaine)

The trumpet slapped by a strong hand
Shines brightly in the morning red and blue,
While with a brash and striking sound
A new tune, louder comes,
Carelessly and confidently, one knows
In the house, where his scent hangs profusely.

Where is this expected grunge
That quickly my rich spirit doth harass?
What would me of you, omnipotent note?
What did you want? Aware, strong, off key?
That in an eternity will keep its spirit
By doorways where the weeds die tragically?

Ladies Look… (Inspired by Rimbaud)

Within him surges the wine of idleness,
Like the sweet deluded harmonica's sigh;
The child can feel, beneath their slow caresses,
Rising, falling, an endless desire to cry.

The pulsating desire to cry out her name,
He dreams of his sister's
Probing, enchanting fingers,
He seeks out her saliva.

In his heavy hair
Surges her red blood.
She tastes like honey
And he pricks her with his rose.

The song is near to an end,
Rising
Falling
No longer a desire.

The Stolen Heart (Inspired by Rimbaud)

My weeping heart on the deck drools spit;
They soil it with cigarette butts,
They splatter it with slop and shit;
My weeping heart on the deck drools spit.
The soldiers drink and laugh at it;
The sound of laughing hurts my guts.
My weeping heart on the deck drools spit;
They soil it with cigarette butts.

Soldiers' cocks are a black burlesque;
They rape my heart with what they say.
In scrawls on the mast, grotesque
Soldiers' cocks are a black burlesque.
Ocean, abra cadabra antesque,
Take my heart and wash it away!
Soldiers' cocks are a black burlesque;
They rape my heart with what they say.

When they are done, and all worn out
How will I act, my stolen heart?
All I will hear is a drunken shout
When they are done and all worn out.
I will throw up and then pass out,
I know, with my heart torn apart

When they are done and all worn out.
How will I act, my stolen heart?

I've found my heart and it will win,
It's bruised and battered in my hands;
Found it out in the trash bin,
I've found my heart and it will win.
I'll encase it in this rusty tin;
Take it away to foreign lands.
I've found my heart and it will win,
It's bruised and battered in my hands!

Flutter

I tilt my head back
And open my mouth
Butterflies, flutter out
I turn my stereo up real loud
But I still cannot
Hear
A sound
I look around but can't see a thing
I open my mouth
I cannot sing
Too many butterflies
Fluttering about
I try to stand
My feet aren't steady
I try to move
I'm just not ready
Too many butterflies
Fluttering about

In View

Do I,
Do I seem lost to you?
Do I,
Do I fall out of view?
Walk off the page
Onto the floor
Across the room
And out the door
Do I, do I seem lost to you?
Do I, do I come into view?
Remind you now
I'm only me
Take me away
I'll let you be
Do I,
Do I seem lost to you?
Do I
Do I fall out of view?
Remind you now
You're still the one
Take me away
We'll still have fun
Do I,
Do I seem sad to you?

Forget About Me

Watching you from afar
I wonder when did you forget about me?
Now that you're Mr High and Mighty
In my living room, on my T.V.
I'm sick of sad, I'm sick of mad
Baby you can always shut me out
She keeps saying that she's fine
He keeps saying next week he'll be slow
The hole in my pocket's getting smaller
The water in the bottle's, well, you know
The photos on the film
The sheets on the line
The T.V's on the windowsill
She keeps persisting
That she's fine
Rents overdue, bills not paid
Baby in the oven and Candy's playing games
Leonard loved his Maryanne
And someone else his Suzy
Baby what I want to know is
When did you forget
About me?

Burning Overtime

The sun is burning overtime
And baby so are you
Hurt feelings permanently
Find out it's you
And here we go again

Listen to your enemies
Find out what they know
Your responsibility
Finally knock you down
And here we go again

Never needing support from you
Never giving in to you
Now I'm left alone
Mad at you for eternity
And here we go again

I search for you and you're not here
I can't find you anywhere
I search for you and see you've gone
You didn't want me all along
And here we go again

Wait and you will see

We were never meant to be
And here we go again
Here we go again
Go again

Turn You On

Don't want to turn you on
Don't want to turn you off
Don't want to turn around
Don't want to go low down

Don't want to tear you up
Don't want to start your fire
Don't want to mess with you
'Coz you're a fucking liar

Don't want to turn you on
Don't want to turn you off.

Another Day

Rain
Falls down outside
It's
Cloudy in my mind
I watch
Your boat sail away
I wait
For another day

My mind's bored
And you're so late
I can't undo
What is our fate
As I watch you drive away
I wait for another day
Another me to go your way
But how long
Shall I
Have to wait?

I didn't want to cry

Lightning
Strikes up in the sky
Why

I love you
I don't know
Why
I only
Wanted to hold her
I didn't
Want to have to go

My mind's bored
And you're so late
I can't undo
What is our fate
As I watch you drive away
I wait for another day
Another me to go your way
But how long shall I
Have to wait?

Next

Where to go next
I'm so glad I found that book
You know the one I wanted
With that little boy on the cover
So bring it on, all those eyes
Look at me, then to the skies
Never coming around for me
Just coming around again
Young lover, young lover
Hands on head, then on breast
Wait for the outsider
Where you going next
Where will you be tomorrow
How can a body be found
And nobody knows who it is?
Where are those that miss them
Or were they a ruby red?